Emotional Intelligence
For Everyone

A Key To Your Personal And Professional Success. Empathetically Handle Your Interpersonal Relationships, Improve Social Skills, Self Management, And Raise Your IQ

By

JACK SMITH

Table of Contents

Introduction

Emotional intelligence is your ability to be aware of emotions, create and enter into feelings, and manage our psychological prosperity to encourage our personal, spiritual and professional growth. The power is if you are fully aware of your emotions and limit your activities and responses, and can very quickly self-inspire and inspire everyone around, developing powerful connections and social skills together and expressing empathy for others.

The twentieth century exposed the chemistry of IQ (intelligence quotient); people's personalities were judged based on an intelligent quotient. In a one-time speech, the ability to eventually become a money-spinner and tune the potential of each luxury entity.

Various studies have indicated that this is a failed practice. Emotional intelligence is required to lead a happy, prosperous and productive life. Although the intelligent quotient is quantified based on certain variables mental age and chronological period, however, psychological wisdom does not have such parameters. It will be improved at a given time in life.

Emotional intelligence is defined by four attributes:

Self-management: You are able to control wrong feelings and behaviors, manage your emotions in a healthy way, take initiative, carry out commitments and adapt to changing circumstances.

Self-Awareness: Recognize your emotions and how they influence your behavior. You recognize your strengths and weaknesses and have confidence in yourself.

Social awareness: you have empathy. You can understand other people's emotions, needs and concerns, catch emotional cues, feel socially comfortable, and recognize the power dynamics in organization.

Relationship Management: You know how to develop good relationships, communicate clearly, and influence others, work well in a team and manage conflicts.

Chapter 1
Why Do We Need Emotions?

Do you consider yourself an emotional or rational person? If you responded emotionally, ask yourself if there were times when you wished you weren't. To be sure, emotions can be very messy. They can make you make the most irrational decisions.

Think about the last time you got crazy. What have you done? Did you end up regretting or wishing you could take it back? You probably have regrets about the course of action you made while you were under emotional tension. You may also be tempted to think that life would be good if we didn't have emotions.

But would it be more natural? Think about it: If your life were all based on logic, you probably wouldn't have any regrets. Each decision would be carefully thought out and calculated to make sure the decision was in everyone's best interest. Relationships would not be based on love; instead, one would enter into a partnership after conducting a thorough evaluation, just as one would do before signing a contract with a seller in a business transaction. There would be no need for fear or sadness. You could rationalize anything and then continue your life without worrying about the constant presence of emotions.

It may sound perfect, but emotions serve a purpose.

It's not just inconveniences or disruptions we face as we try to live our best life. Instead, emotions are an essential component of survival. Put simply; emotions are the flow of information between you and external stimuli. Without passion, you would not be able to read your environment and respond appropriately correctly. Without an adequate response, you would struggle to overcome any environmental challenges you may encounter.

Suppose, for example; you are a 15-year-old going about your business in the school lobby when the resident bully comes at you showering jokes and blows. An expected emotional response, in this case, would be anger. When you are angry, your body goes into combat mode. This is how your brain protects you. Getting angry could save you from enduring more insults from this horrible human being.

In addition to helping us thrive and stay out of harm's way, emotions also help us communicate. Think about it: If your significant other is upset about something you did, you need to understand that what you did was upsetting to them. If you are a right partner, you will avoid doing this in the future out of respect for your significant others feelings. Emotions are part of how we tell our truth to other people, and vice versa.

Emotions are also part of our identity. Are you a happy person or an angry person? You'd be surprised how people come to define you based on the emotion you usually give to the world. Whether this is actually who you are is a question for another day. You can likely name one or two colleagues who you consider happy people or angry people depending on the emotion you often feel they feel. Emotions, therefore, play a significant role in how others see us.

To understand emotions further, some researchers have tried to understand the various roles played by different emotions. Typically, these researchers will focus on the most common emotions experienced by most people around the world, regardless of their cultural or socioeconomic background.

The fundamental emotions

The desire to understand emotions dates back to ancient times when scholars such as the Greek philosopher Aristotle advanced their theories about the nature and purpose of emotions. Aristotle believed that feelings were an essential component of moral excellence. William James, an American philosopher and psychologist, had a different view of emotions. He argued that emotions are the result of the human body undergoing various physiological changes related to the external environment.

In the period between Aristotle's time and today, there have been several theories put forward by psychologists and scientists who have tried to explain where emotions come from and why they are essential. Robert Plutchik, professor and psychologist, have conceptualized one of the most popular methods. Plutchik invented the emotion wheel (known as Plutchik's wheel of emotions), which shows that there are eight primary emotions from which all other emotions come. In this wheel, conflicting emotions are mapped against each other. For example, joy is contrasted with sadness, while surprise is juxtaposed with anticipation. The eight-core emotions included in

Plutchik's wheel of emotions are the happiest emotions of joy, trust,

Why are some people more emotional than others?

If humans feel the same kind of emotions, then why do some people seem more emotional than others? Highly emotional or highly sensitive people are easy to spot. While everyone else seems to process information and emotions fleetingly, these individuals bask in their feelings for longer than is sometimes comfortable. They may cry out loud during sad movie scenes, open their homes to stray animals, or quickly feel offended by things people do or say, even if there was no intention of offending. It's easy to think of a highly sensitive person as being overly dramatic when it comes to their actions and emotions. The truth is this is not a cry for attention,

The study of emotions is nowhere near being fully explored. Scientists are still in the relatively newer stages of exploring feelings and how people's genetic makeup affects them. Therefore, it will take some time for a consensus to be reached on specific topics such as highly sensitive people and so on. That said, there have been studies that have shown that how a person reacts to their environment is the result of some form of genetic conditioning.

One such study was conducted by researcher Rachael Grazioplene and her colleagues in 2012 and subsequently published in Child Psychology and Psychiatry. During this research, Grazioplene and her team focused on the cholinergic system. The cholinergic system is the body system that regulates the kind of attention we give to the environment around us and how we process the information we get from these environments. The results of this showed that a particular type of receptor gene referred to as CHRNA4 (of the cholinergic system) can affect how one behaves emotionally depending on the kind of nourishment this person receives. As such, the interaction between this gene and think about it: if you grew up in a family where emotions are nothing to be ashamed of, you would most likely grow up believing and practising the same. If you grew up hugging your parents and siblings, chances are you will also be very affectionate with other people when you are an adult. As such, you may be born with a sensitive gene, but until your environment encourages it to thrive, you may find yourself repressing your feelings. Conversely, a person who was born with a fragile gene and was raised in a highly nutritious environment will have no problem being highly expressive emotionally.

At the same time, it is good to note that some people may feel the pressure to act emotionally because of what their culture expects them to be. More elaboration on the same can be found in chapter 7, where we mention that women are more emotional than men.

What are the benefits of EI

It is a false notion that psychological Intellect is only needed in the social arena, such as developing an excellent long-term relationship with others; however, it has a significant part of the performance in every part of life. The considerable benefits of emotional intelligence are: -

Stress Relief - During our Conducted Emotional Intelligence Certificate each year, we focus enormously on explaining the significance of emotional intelligence in releasing stress, stress and anxiety and achieving superior health.

Power to face failure and complaint absolutely - You will not find praise and more complaints in life. An IE knows its strengths and areas to use. He chooses criticism and failure another step towards victory.

What is emotional intelligence and how to benefit from it? There is a significant range of definitions to achieve this. Most individuals will define this as an art in which someone can synchronize their thoughts, and the human body behaves through acts of mind control; some specify the subject due to higher air instincts that help a person respond to the situation. These people are right; some other person who realizes emotional intelligence creates tons of benefits in their life. It is essential to understand that a standard individual includes a particular level of mental knowledge; however, people can train their heads to get high amounts with art.

For anyone interested in realizing the mental Intellect, later developing the ideal mental attitude before engaging in these defining behaviours, a person is likely to be most prosperous from art. An individual needs to build visualization systems that are effective in bringing about the kind of success they would like to achieve. An individual should also seek advice on how he can control or better make the most of international legislation to influence the desired effect. Contrary to what many believe, the laws of appeal have become fundamental to forming a single personality. Individuals who encourage erroneous thoughts to the public that they find most frequently do not need an extremely negative character that liberates a good life in general.

It is essential to understand that achieving personal improvement acts in virtually any section of life is not just a one day task. An individual must remain consistent and continuous in almost any private improvement action to achieve specified success. The degree to which self-improvement success is achieved will likely be quantified by the campaigns someone is ready to carry out to get what they want.

Individuals who have achieved mental brain visual effects have many benefits employed for them, for example, it is exceptionally feasible for people who have made such success, Exude acts as telepathy, mind-reading and maybe even healing skills. The skill of their heads. There is no limit to what an individual can achieve. By changing the capacity of one's head, it is only necessary that anyone generate an Interest and also a belief system that can accomplish the things they want to achieve. Through electricity in the minds. As previously mentioned before, visualizing an excuse of What is emotional intelligence, people may have different thoughts and notions towards different meanings. But,

The three models

All of these three main types of mental intelligence bring a whole new position within people's emotional attachment in their daily activity and thus form the cornerstone. These generally include the capacity model, the mixed version, and also the attribute model. We focus on David Goleman's mixed model.

The six-second style of emotional intelligence is just a framework of the procedure for obtaining and using feelings efficiently. Unlike other theoretical models, this is an incremental, practical and straightforward procedure that facilitates performance. The original version, on the left, can be a cycle of three critical activities.

Chapter 2
Essential Facts Of Emotional Intelligence

What is Emotion, and where does it come from?

Emotion is the instinctive mood resulting from external or internal stimuli. In the 20th century, 6 basic emotions were decided by a psychologist named Paul Ekman. I am disgust, anger, sadness, joy, fear and surprise. There are, of course, many emotions not mentioned in these six, but most of them will be experienced for a lifetime. It is said that our human emotions may be the result of evolution. Disgust, for example, is what we teach our children to feel when they are around a dirty garbage can or when they want to eat a piece of spoiled food.

Speaking of evolutionary emotions, have you ever opened a drawer on a spider or stepped on a snake. The excitement of surprise is what tells our body to move away from creatures that might bite us quickly. It is fear that prevents us from putting ourselves in situations that will put us in danger. For each of these emotions, there is a dedicated circuit in our brain, and it derives from a complex system of feelings and reactions.

These emotions are called "primary emotions". There are also, on the contrary, complicated emotions. Some of these complex emotions are humility, shame, nostalgia and guilt. These emotions are mostly learned emotions and work more socially than for survival. Complex emotions also have their distinct circuits in the brain and are more common in the later years of one's life.

Because these feelings have such a significant effect on how we think and behave, scientists have spent time trying to understand them. Thoughts cause our emotions. Often an external stimulus will cause us internally to think about the best reaction in response to how we feel about it. Even though multiple people may be in the same boat, they will most likely differ in how they think about it. This can be based on previous learning and experience. For example, if you and your friend have gone to the lake to swim, your friend who has never swum in a lake before may fear being bitten by a fish. However, you have already swum in a lake, and you know that the fish in the pond will not bother you.

We know that certain emotions are the result of certain types of thoughts, such as when we think, "I feel like I'm in danger," we feel fear in response. When we imagine something terrible happening to us, we are also afraid. Scientists have established that these types of thoughts are what prepare us for our future. When we practice the response in our daily life, we are better preparing ourselves for situations that will arise in our later lives, such as loss or anger. These types of questions have been found by scientists to answer questions like;

- Was what happened unexpected?

- Will I be able to cope with what happened?

- Will, what happened make it easier or harder for me to get what I want?

- Is what happened funny?

- Does what happened to coincide with what I think is right and wrong?

- Was what happened my fault or someone else's?

This is where we begin to look at our situations in a more positive light. It will make us feel sad when our ice cream machine breaks down, but we will most likely feel a lot more disturbing when we think there is nothing we can do to fix it. We can look at it more positively, however, and realize that there are probably a lot of resources online that can show us how to fix our ice cream machine.

There is a unique phenomenon that I haven't mentioned yet called "unconscious processing". Unconscious processing occurs when you experience emotion but are not sure why. Our brains work a lot and do many things when we are not paying attention. We don't notice most of what he is doing every day, and this includes triggering an emotion. It's a foolish thought that your brain notices things that you cannot consciously see happening, but that happens. If you find yourself feeling a certain way and aren't sure why you think this way, try thinking about what's happening around you ... what's happening.

Unconscious emotions are a big part of why we have psychiatrists today to talk about how we feel. A psychiatrist is a person trained to listen to you and interpret your feelings in a way that you may not have seen before. It's wise to get an outside opinion on anything, and a psychiatrist can help you cope with things like loss, the grief of a loved one, guilt, or trauma.

According to scientists, an "emotional reaction" has several parts. These parts don't necessarily occur in any order, but they do happen when a new emotion is experienced. Maybe your brain will change the way your body works first. When one is "in pain," often the typical response is to drop to one's knees or need to sit down. Pain is a powerful emotion and requires a lot of concentration. When in mourning, the brain automatically prioritizes feeling that passion and nothing else seems to matter. There are also positive reactions caused by the brain, such as smiling when you are happy and laughing when you are amused.

Another part of an emotional reaction is your brain, making you think differently or focus on individual thoughts. When you are happy, your mind will concentrate on easy ideas and things that bring you joy or make you smile, and when you are sad, you may feel the urge to listen to sad music or focus on anxious thoughts. Think about the last time you remember being afraid. When you felt like you were in danger, do you remember that your brain was looking for other dangerous things? It is comparable to being on a roller coaster and being afraid of the tracks breaking. You start wincing with every creak you hear and every bump you hear. Your brain consciously makes you feel like you are in danger, and you need to be ultra-aware of your surroundings.

The third part of your reaction may be the feelings and impulses you try to act or act differently than you usually do when you experience an intense emotion such as fear or anger. You can scream or scream. This too, can be a part of depression. You may feel as if you want to stay closed in your home and avoid contact with the outside world.

Emotions come from your brain and are the result of being a human being. Human beings are unique in all of nature due to the complex emotions we experience. They help us interact socially with others and survive. There are many parts to an emotional reaction, and your feelings may be conscious or subconsciously felt, but overall we know there are positive ways to deal with them.

Before delving into what emotional intelligence is and how it works, you must first learn to understand the concepts behind it. Each person experiences emotions and has a unique temperament, and most people experience empathy in some way. These combine and create your reactions to emotionally unstable situations. Each of these is closely related to emotional intelligence, and having an understanding of what causes them and why we have them is key to increasing it. By knowing how these relate to emotional intelligence, you can work with them instead of against them, seeing much faster progress than going blind. Those with low EQ are typically slaves to their temperaments and emotions and react as such,

Understanding of emotions

There are different human emotions; all made up of basic emotions that can combine into a broad spectrum of what one feels from day to day. It is believed that emotions can be reduced to four underlying feelings: happiness, sadness, anger and fear. Every emotion you may experience, from surprise to guilt or disgust, are all subsets of those four emotions. These four are believed to be biologically rooted in us through evolution, although more nuanced or complicated feelings can be developed through sociological sources, such as cultural influence.

The purpose of emotions

These four emotions must be necessary if they have evolved to be universal: almost any human being of any culture can see the image of another human being making one of these four expressions and know precisely what it is. The reason for this is to be able to communicate quickly and clearly with other human beings. By developing both expressions of universal emotion, humans pave the way for the development of empathy as well.

Each of the four universal emotions conveys something different: they identify different situations and needs. Happiness communicates that all requirements are met. Sadness informs that something terrible has happened or that something or someone famous has been lost or damaged and indicates that there is a need for support to encourage healing. Anger conveys the feeling of being wronged, whether taken advantage of or betrayed and suggests the need for limitations or protection. Fear communicates that there is a threat or danger nearby and that safety is needed.

As a social species, we need to be able to communicate our basic needs to ensure that everyone's needs are met. If we don't know how our neighbours are doing, we never know if they need additional help or support, or if we are pissing them off and need to step back. Through communication, everyone's needs are met more efficiently, and the easiest way to communicate those needs is through universal body language. With body language and emotions, we can see, at a glance, how people around us are feeling. We can also tell the intentions of strangers by being able to see signs of anger on their expressions, or whether they are happy, scared or sad. Communicate at a glance

Emotions also have internal connotations. These can encourage or motivate us to act in specific ways, as well as aiding overall survival. If you are afraid, your body prepares to flee or fight to keep you alive. If you are angry, your body adjusts to protect itself. Happiness causes relaxation and encourages you to engage in more behaviours that triggered happiness, to begin with. Sadness helps us to protect those we love or change our situations into something that brings us joy.

The cause of emotions

There are several theories about what causes emotions, but the three most common are the James-Lange theory, the Cannon-Bard theory, and the Schacter-Singer model. Each of these is slightly different and offers various explanations.

The James-Lange theory believes that emotion is a person's understanding of the physiological changes the body creates in response to a stimulus. If a person sees a snake and feels its extremities start tingling, their heartbeats wildly, and their breathing quickens as they focus on the snake in front of them, they know that what they are physically feeling is fear and respond in that way. In this theory, physical changes come first, and the mind labels material changes as emotions to understand them.

The Cannon-Bard theory believes that we perceive things around us with our five senses, and the observed information is sent through the nervous system to the brain, where two different parts receive the message. The cortex, or the front of the mind, gets a signal and responds to the news while the hypothalamus receives a second copy of the word and creates the physical reactions. In this case, the man sees the snake. His eyes send the message that he saw a snake to both the cortex and the hypothalamus.

The cortex creates the emotion in response to the stimulus while the hypothalamus creates the physical response. Physical and emotional responses combine to create a feeling of fear.

The Schacter-Singer model believes that fear is a combination of physical responses to a stimulus coupled with conscious thoughts about the stimulus. The two together create a general feeling towards the stimulus, which is interpreted as emotion. For example, the man who has seen a snake may feel his heartbeat speed up in response to the snake, but his feelings depend on his cognitive thoughts on the idea of snakes. If he believes snakes are quite charming and loves to watch them, that accelerated heart rate can be interpreted as happiness. Still, if he has learned that snakes should be avoided at all costs, that same pulse increase combined with those beliefs would create a feeling of fear.

James-Lange theory

Emotion is a person's interpretation of physical changes in the body in response to a stimulus

Cannon-bard theory

The body sends information from the senses to the cortex, which creates emotions, and to the hypothalamus of the brain, which creates physical responses such as crying or shaking in fear.

SchacterSinger Model

Emotion is created when physical changes and conscious thoughts are combined about a stimulus

Conflict of rationality versus emotionality

Often, in our mind, we are continually hovering somewhere between the rational and the emotional. The emotional part of our brain was born first, designed to keep us alive long enough to reproduce.

The sensible part of our mind is what makes us distinctly human: it allows us to act in ways that are contradictory to our emotions to achieve a better result. We let emotions to influence our thoughts and decisions, but we allow the rational part of our mind to control the emotional component to keep it in balance. To be successful people, especially in the workplace and in relationships, we need a healthy balance between rationality and emotionality. Sometimes, however, we find our sense of rationality stifled by the emotional side of our mind. In this case, the person would be entirely enslaved by emotions. Consider that the person who is afraid of snakes has a phobia of the snake and, seeing a harmless garden snake crawling in front of him, panic and freezes from sight. In this case, it was governed by his emotions; his rational side of the brain, which would have reminded him that the snake is tiny and harmless, has been silenced by the feeling of fear. His emotions governed him; his rational side of the brain, which would have reminded him that the snake is tiny and harmless, has been silenced by the feeling of fear. His emotions governed him; his rational side of the brain, which would have reminded him that the snake is tiny and harmless, has been silenced by the feeling of fear.

The relevance of emotions for emotional intelligence

This battle of rationality and emotionality relates directly to emotional intelligence: it is the ability to identify those emotions, manage them and balance them in such a way as to allow for rational thinking. A high EQ means that you are likely to be adept at managing your emotions and giving them the consideration they deserve while keeping them in check and allowing rationality to rule. This allows for stability, which helps the man who is afraid of snakes to walk away merely slightly upset at seeing a snake, but still fully capable of functioning.

Chapter 3
Understanding Empathy

Empathy is the ability to know and feel another person's feelings as if you were experiencing them yourself. Understanding allows you to take a look at a grieving widow and feel her pain strong enough to motivate you to help her, or this will enable you to contact proud and happy for your son who joined the college basketball team when comes to tell you the good news, his face lights up with pure joy.

There are five critical components of empathy: understanding others, developing others, service orientation, exploiting diversity, and political awareness. These together combine to create the understanding you feel for others. It's a skill that can be developed, although it should come naturally to some degree.

Understanding others

It involves the perception of the feelings of others and an interest in any concerns or needs of the other person.

Develop others

It involves action to satisfy other people's needs or feelings

Service orientation

It involves putting others first and trying to go out of your way to help people.

Leverage diversity

Recognize both the differences between people's abilities and the value of diversity for the survival of the group

Political awareness

It involves the response to the emotional states of a group, allowing you to foster a group relationship

The purpose of empathy

Empathy exists to keep us aware of the needs of others. We use insight to allow us to look at a person close to us and understand how they are feeling, which in turn makes us know what that person might need at that particular moment. By following how someone thinks through empathy, we can relate to other people within our social groups, and this motivates us to help them meet their needs. It instils in us this sense of compassion that encourages us to care for others and to behave selflessly. This altruism allows more substantial groups of people to survive. It is that inherent desire to ensure that your partners, friends, children, and other loved ones are cared for, which further helps ensure their survival.

 Empathy goes a step further in ensuring survival as well: it allows you to adapt work to the strengths of individuals, fully expecting that each contributes to the survival of society in a meaningful way. Instead of each person having to go out and survive alone without help, empathy, and community allow each person to specialize. One person can hunt while another focuses on agriculture and yet other works on the construction and general maintenance of the village. Someone else can ultimately produce the food that the hunter and farmer provide and, eventually, everyone is left with a variety of needs satisfied while having to specialize in one task.

The doctor doesn't have to worry about hunting to make sure he has food so he can focus on medical care. The hunter does not have to worry about making clothes, so he can focus solely on providing food. The teacher does not have to worry about food or shelter and can look after the children instead. In today's society, it takes a village to satisfy all needs and empathy is what allows us to do that.

Empathy and emotional intelligence

Empathy is one of the main components of emotional intelligence. Compassion serves as a bond between you and those around you, and that ability to understand those around you as if you were in their shoes. This allows you to deepen your bonds with other people, which can be the key to building a higher EQ. Consider the angry man who came home from work mentioned in the introduction: if he stopped and considered how the person he had been arguing with at work had felt, he could have responded better. If the two had quarrelled over a part of their work that was not completed because each believed that the other would take care of it, the man could have stopped to consider that maybe his colleague had been confused and it was all a big misunderstanding. Through empathy, you can better control your emotions because you are aware of how they affect those around you. You can see and feel the pain you inflict when you act impulsively or out of anger or fear. Likewise, you feel good when the people around you feel good, making you more interested in meeting the needs of others.

Understanding of temperamen

Temperament describes the nature of an individual: it is the way he behaves naturally. It is mainly inherited genetically, creating traits that were nurtured or developed early in life, or that came innately. Temperament is particularly complicated as it is a predisposition for a specific type of behaviour, although it does not necessarily guarantee that everything you are predisposed to will happen. Here are four examples of temperament in action:

Timid

Quiet, uncomfortable in groups, avoid being the center of attention

Stubborn

Stubborn, refuses to compromise, refuses to admit he's wrong

Athletic

Competitive, active, strong, team player

Outgoing

Enjoys attention, thrives with friends, seeks out many social situations

The purpose of temperament

Temperament provides your core personality. It's your inherent preferences and dislikes, how you react to crowds if you like sports, how you respond to certain stimuli, and so much more. Your temperament is essentially the necessary foundation of your personality. You can be introverted or outgoing, athletic, stubborn, easy-going, submissive, or with many other different traits. Temperament serves that basis and determines our reactions. Someone shy is unlikely to enjoy a school prom and will likely do whatever it takes to jump or leave early.

In contrast, someone who is stubborn and dominant will likely thrive in some sort of leadership position and actively avoid anything. Situations that would require a presentation. Your temperament prompts other people to respond to you in a certain way, while you probably get the same cues from other people's character. The critical part to remember is that while you can shape your temperament, you can't completely change it. While your personality influences your behaviour, what it does is determine how you do something rather than what you choose to do. Your temper isn't an excuse for misbehaviour, but it will provide you with information to understand why you have the tendencies you have. What it does is determine how you do something rather than what you choose to do. Your temper is no excuse for misbehaviour, but it will provide you with information to understand why you have the tendencies you have. What it does is determine how you do something rather than what you choose to do. Your temper is no excuse for misbehaviour, but it will provide you with information to understand why you have the tendencies you have.

The cause of temperament

Temperament is believed to be largely inherited, but it is also related to the environment you may be in and even to life experience, particularly in the younger years. Genetic or biological predispositions, physical attributes, background, and early life experiences all come together to form your temperament. Someone with a natural inclination to caution or anxiety which was born into a stressful environment and spent much of early childhood crying, as their parents claimed, is likely to become an anxious person. In contrast, that same child could generally have been happy but somehow cautious or slow to prepare for situations if the parents had been less combative and the home more relaxed and encouraging in the early years. All in all,

The importance of temperament for emotional intelligence

Those with lower EQs are typically slaves to their temperament. Their EQ may not be sufficient to mitigate harmful or destructive behaviours, and they react emotionally rather than rationally. They will almost always behave in ways that come naturally due to their temperament. This is not still a good thing: the shy person becomes unable to overcome his fear of social events and may have difficulties in professional or academic settings.

The stubborn person can ruin relationships because they are not entirely willing to compromise or admit when they are wrong. These can lead to catastrophic results where people are unsuccessful and dissatisfied with their life, and the people around them are just as unhappy.

On the other hand, people with higher levels of emotional intelligence can more or less override their core temperaments. Although, on the whole, they are still shy or stubborn, they can get over those temperaments to do what they need to.

The shy person can be a fantastic HR director, despite hating social interaction, because he can look beyond the anxiety he feels when confronted with people or problems and instead, with empathy and compassion, decides to help others people rather than yielding their introverted nature to her The stubborn man may hate to admit. Still, he is willing to do so when he can rationalize that he is wrong. By having higher levels of emotional intelligence, people can recognize their feelings and temperament for who they are but can use the rational part of their mind to overcome them when needed or when it is helpful to do so.

Chapter 4
Importance Of Emotional Intelligence

You may be wondering why emotional intelligence is essential. If you can innately understand basic emotions and those emotions have particular purposes, why is it is vital that you can influence them? If they are evolutionarily significant, why ignore them? Wouldn't that be counterproductive to our very nature as human beings? Yes and no; emotions are essential and should be taken into account as they often have significant implications, but at the same time, if all we do is give in to our emotions, which are, after all, quite fickle, we become impulsive and unproductive. Relationships suffer when we respond to people because we were momentarily angry with them. We say things with anger that we may not mean. Sadness and pain can be utterly paralyzing if we act accordingly. Happiness and fun can lead to destructive behaviours like drug abuse, but they can also destroy careers if everything you do is what makes you happy regardless of responsibilities. Fear can make you paralyzed when what you need to do is take action to save yourself or others you care about.

These emotions are biologically relevant, but humans have developed to the point where we can think critically and rationally. If we only react based on emotions, we would paralyze our potential. Think about how a child behaves - he is likely impulsive and gives in to every passing sensation, as that's all he knows. He doesn't know how to control his emotions, and his need for instant gratification leads to all kinds of problems. Young children may hit, scream, throw tantrums, steal, or impulsively endanger themselves. They do not have the capacity for rational thinking that humans develop in early adulthood. To deny that rationality and to refuse to act on it is to deny humanity itself.

Being able to influence all your behaviours with rational thinking means that you are not a slave to instinct. You can act selflessly to help someone else, even if your instincts are screaming at you to leave. You can be a leader who recognizes the feelings of everyone around you and leads with compassion and empathy rather than domination. Your behaviours are the keys to all interpersonal relationships. When you can control those behaviours with high EQ, you can better influence your relationships and be more successful in social situations. A high EQ allows you to be more efficient at resolving conflicts and empathize with others. By having better relationships with those around you, you are more likely to be happy and relaxed.

Ultimately, there isn't a single aspect of your life that isn't touched in some way by emotional intelligence. It affects everything, whether you are aware of it or not. EQ affects your success both socially and professionally; sometimes more than IQ and understanding its importance is key to understanding why developing a higher EQ is so crucial to success in life.

Applications of emotional intelligence

Understanding how EQ can affect various aspects of relationships is key to seeing how deeply it can impact your life. This section will provide what a high EQ looks like in each of the following situations and compare it to what might happen when someone with a lower EQ is also in the same location. The difference between the two can be astounding when compared side by side.

EQ in romantic relationships

Imagine that you and your spouse are arguing again. Your spouse is a stay-at-home parent for young children as you work full time during standard office hours. Every day you come home, and your spouse asks for help as soon as you walk in the door. You can see your spouse looking stressed out, still wearing dirty pyjamas, dinner is on the stove, cooking and living room looks like a toy bomb exploded. The kids are arguing, and your spouse quickly pushes the kids towards you and hands you the spatula before disappearing into the bathroom, closing and closing the door and opening the shower.

Assuming you have a lower EQ, you may immediately get angry. After all, you have just come home from work and are mentally drained from a working day in the office. Your spouse has to stay home, you tell yourself angrily, and it seems like your spouse hasn't done anything all day. The house is destroyed, the children are not fed, and the dinner is not over. In your anger, you follow your spouse to the bathroom and proceed to scream through the door. You don't recognize that your spouse seemed stressed before leaving or you think that all your spouse had heard all day was the sound of kids' bickering that was escalating your anger. Babies listen to you scream from the door and run away crying. Your spouse does not open the door. Dinner burns on the stove. All of this aggravates your anger and makes the situation worse. Your relationships with both your spouse and your children have been damaged. Your spouse feels like you are not supportive, and your children learn to avoid you because you are an angry person.

Stop and think about how the situation would have turned out if you had had a higher EQ. You would walk in the door and see the despair painted on your spouse's face. You would have been able to feel the stress and anxiety practically coming from your spouse and see how overwhelmed your spouse was with the situation. Instead of getting angry, you would have seen that what your spouse needed was a quick respite from the constant annoyance of children. You would have happily entertained the children, and the change of pace may have been enough to stop their disputes. You would have finished dinner, serving it up and serving the children, who ran happily to eat. Your spouse would have come out of the shower feeling much more comfortable and ready to face the rest of the evening, and you would have felt supported and loved because you took the initiative to relieve some stress. Your relationship, instead of being hurt, was strengthened by your ability to scale the situation. Also, your children learn that marriage is a partnership. The random comparison is harmful, and what a marriage needs is for both partners to take care of each other's needs, even when they are not verbally expressed and even when they may not be convenient.

EQ in family relationships

Imagine that your children have been misbehaving all day. They keep running around the house like children do when they are locked up in the house due to bad weather, and no matter how often you tell them to stop, you can hear the sound of their quick footsteps running down the hall again a few minutes later. After reminding them to stay for the umpteenth time and enjoy the momentary relief from the constant blows of the feet, their rush is heard starting again, followed by a loud bang and the glass shattering. Run outside and see that your kids, because they weren't listening, ran into the hutch and knocked out a whole row of wine glasses, which shattered all over the floor.

Assuming you have low EQ, chances are you wind up and scream. You immediately yell at the children for not listening to them, chewing on them for the disobedience that ruined everything and telling them to look at the mess they left you. Despite the fear, pain and guilt on their faces, you belittle them for not listening, say something along the lines of accusing them of not being good guys or wishing they weren't there, and yelling at both of them to go to theirs. Rooms for the rest of the night. Your children stare at you in horror for a moment before bursting into tears and running away. You ignored the fact that one of the kids had a cut in their foot and the other was terrified of you, and you ignored the damage your outburst has had on your kids. As your children get older,

With a higher EQ, you would have run out to see what happened and immediately ask if your kids are okay. You would go through them, grab each of them from the glass and take them to the other room to patch them up while you had a serious, but still calm conversation about why you asked them not to play so brutally indoors. Instead of losing your temper, you used the accident to teach the children a lesson. When they were all patched up, you brought them back to clutter and asked them to help you clean it up in an age-appropriate way. Each child contributed to the chaos, and each of them sincerely apologized. You hugged your kids, reminded them that you love them, and sternly told them to avoid running around the house. They nodded and went off to play alone, feeling secure in their attachment to you, and having learned a precious lesson. You have strengthened your relationship with your children, and they have learned that they can count on you in times of need thanks to your balanced response to what used to be a messy situation.

EQ in platonic relationships

Imagine getting ready to have your friend come over to your house for an evening of video games, a few beers and some pizza. It's a low-key event meant to be relaxing. The time your friend was supposed to arrive came and went, and almost an hour later, he finally shows up. He seems upset about something and mumbles apologies, but completely avoids the subject of why he was late. Instead, he grabs a beer, sits quietly and watches you play. He drinks the beer and then takes another without saying a word. He turns the phone off and on again, his expression darkening every time he does.

If you have a lower EQ, you may respond negatively. You're hurt that your friend was late and didn't offer an apology or explanation. You are angry because you feel devalued. You're sad that your friend doesn't seem to care that you feel upset about his actions. Instead of looking at him and seeing his feelings, you look at him and snap. You tell him that if he doesn't want to be there, and it seems like he is, then he can just walk away because you don't need his negativity to lower the mood when you wanted to have fun. You scold him for checking his phone so often and tell him he's a bad friend and you refuse to put up with such disrespect. In response, your friend doesn't say a word. He picks up the phone, looks like he might cry and walks away. He texts you again never responds when you call and refuses to recognize you every time you see him around. He ended the friendship for your outburst.

With a higher EQ, you may have looked at the situation and seen that your friend was not doing well. At first glance, you would have been able to see the pain in his expression upon entering your door and would have been more willing to provide him with the support he needed. Despite the annoyance you felt, you also realized that your friend was unwell and this replaced your annoyance. Even if he didn't want to talk about what had happened, you would have seen that what he needed right now was to be supported during some sort of personal struggle. Instead of putting it down, you would have patiently waited for him to share what happened, and while you expected, you would have continued to play and genuinely enjoy your friend's company. Finally,

EQ in workplace relationships

Imagine you are at work. You have a group project that you and your colleagues have been working on in the last month. The day before the project presentation, you all realize that no one has worked on a specific part of the project that was incredibly important and without it, your project cannot be presented. Each of you thought another person would complete that part of the project and no one checked it until the day before the deadline when you were putting the project together so that you could review the final project. The last piece of the project takes a long time.

With lower EQ, you could explode on your peers. You can shout that it's not done and blame other people around you, looking for any explanation that removes the blame from yourself. You say it was your colleague Mary's fault because she should have done something else related to it. You may yell out some words that aren't appropriate in the workplace and get you in trouble with HR. The assignment is never carried out. Also, you are all reprimanded for failing to meet the requirements and find yourself without a job due to the situation escalating so severely.

With a higher EQ, you may be angry, and you may have seen the frustration on everyone else's faces, but instead of giving in to that anger and frustration, you've chosen to analyze the situation instead. You've looked at what was still needed, and while it would be a lot for a single person to complete, point out that it's something you can all finish relatively quickly if everyone takes a portion of it. Everyone in your group looks to you to listen to you, and soon the mood seems to calm down. Your colleagues follow your lead, and within a few hours, you have completed the remaining work together. Your project is submitted on time, and everyone is thrilled with the result. You feel happy and satisfied because you managed to turn a bad situation into a good one, and your colleagues feel like you are trustworthy and like they can count on you when things get tough. The next time you all have a project, you are appointed the leader who is responsible for making sure everyone has a role, and everything is completed. This newfound admiration from peers improves your reputation with your bosses, and you soon find yourself with a raise and promotion thanks to your tact and emotional intelligence.

EQ in social situations

Imagine you are at a big party. You've always been a little more reserved and hate going to events like this, but one of your friends pushed you to attend. The party is loud, hateful, and everyone around you is drinking, something you don't feel comfortable doing in public. A person walks by, clearly intoxicated, and trips and spills a beer on your shirt. Shout excuses and continue on his way, leaving you drenched in beer in the middle of a party you didn't want to attend.

With a lower EQ, you can look at your friend for a moment before exploding. You scream at how you didn't want to join the party in the first place. Tell your friend that next time he should listen to you and throw down the drink he was given before going out. Quickly, the party seems to settle down as all eyes are on you. They watch you as you leave and the party seems to go down. Your friend watches awkwardly as you leave, and in the next few days, the news of your outburst in the middle of the party spreads among your peers, tarnishing your reputation. People stop wanting to talk to you or invite you to places, and the friend you yelled at seems less interested in continuing your friendship.

With a higher level of EQ, you may have stopped, got frustrated, but then recognized that it was an accident. You wouldn't have let your previous annoyance not want to be there blowing you up. Instead, you would have quietly apologized for cleaning without making a scene or destroying someone's floor at a party.

You would have found something to do with your friend, and you would have tried to have fun, even if you would have preferred to do something else. By not getting sucked into your anger, you are still able to find joy in other things. You may also be able to make new friends or try new things. Regardless of whether you eventually find something useful, by not reacting volatile, you can avoid overreacting and hurting the people around you.

Chapter 5

The Emotional Intelligence Framework

Emotional intelligence is made up of several skills that enable you to understand and evaluate emotions, regardless of whether they are yours or belong to other people. People with higher EQs are typically much more effective at controlling and regulating their feelings, which allows people to control behaviours better.

Break down emotional intelligence

Emotional intelligence is best understood by breaking it down beyond understanding what it is as a whole. The totality of emotional intelligence is made up of five separate realms of emotional intelligence, which are further organized into four quadrants that influence each other. Understanding these ways of breaking down and organizing emotional intelligence is helpful in understanding where you are and what the purpose of each skill is.

Realms of emotional intelligence

Emotional intelligence skills can be divided into five realms or separate behaviours and abilities:

- *Understanding your emotions*

- *Regulate your emotions*

- *Keep yourself motivated*

- *Understanding and recognizing other people's emotions*

- *Manage relationships* (manage other people's feelings)

Each of these realms of emotional intelligence is important, but being secure in one doesn't necessarily mean you're emotionally intelligent, nor does it mean you'll be particularly useful in social situations. To be emotionally intelligent, you need to be competent in all five realms. Someone who understands and controls his emotions without regard for the feelings of others will not be emotionally intelligent; all he will do is to make sure his needs are met. Likewise, someone who is adept at understanding and recognizing the emotions of others but is terrible at self-regulating emotions will be disinterested and will find that their needs are never met. All five realms come together to create a well-rounded, emotionally intelligent person.

Emotional intelligence quadrants

The four quadrants or domains of emotional intelligence are:

- *Self-awareness*

- *Self-management*

- *Social awareness*

- *Relationship management*

As you can see, each of these is closely related to one of the realms of emotional intelligence. Each of these skills can be sorted on a chart to represent a different combination of self or socio-relational and awareness or regulation.

Each quadrant of emotional intelligence is closely related to the others. High self-awareness typically lends itself to greater social awareness and self-management. When you have more significant social knowledge and self-management, you are more likely to have more top relationship management skills.

When all four quadrants are highly developed, that person is believed to be very emotionally intelligent.

Self-awareness

Within emotional intelligence, self-awareness involves developing a deeper understanding of one's emotions. It consists in knowing yourself and understanding what you feel or need. If you can identify and meet your own needs, you are much more likely to understand and meet other people's needs. For this reason, the foundation of emotional intelligence begins with self-awareness.

Some traits associated with self-awareness include the following:

Be confident because you understand yourself

Be aware of your strengths and weaknesses

Be mindful of your current emotional state

Understanding how your actions affect other people

Understand and be mindful of how other people or situations affect your emotional state

By having a deep understanding of yourself, you have the foundation for understanding others. After all, if you couldn't identify when you are sad, how could you hope to recognize sadness in another person? Without the most fundamental foundations of emotions and how they impact you, you will struggle to relate to other people truly.

Low self-awareness

Several signs could indicate that you have a low self-awareness quotient. If you feel you have any of these signs, you must need to work on your self-awareness.

Easily Stressed Out: When you're not in control of your emotions and don't do what's necessary to cope with negative ones, you may find yourself easily stressed out by things that wouldn't be a big deal for someone with a higher EQ. If you are not dealing with your emotions when they arise due to a lack of knowledge to do so, you will see that they build up and stress you out.

Difficulty being assertive: People who lack the necessary EQ often struggle to manage conflict productively. Instead, they resort to passive or aggressive behaviours to push through the battle.

Struggle to describe emotional states: People who can't label specific emotions as they feel them struggle to manage them. For example, while they may be able to identify that they are feeling bad, they cannot label whether what they are experiencing is anxiety, frustration, or sadness.

Acting on assumptions: People without EQ often make a sudden decision or guess and then fall victim to the error of confirmation bias; they will accept any evidence to support their opinion while ignoring the evidence that contradicts it.

Holding Grudges: Grudges stem from stress responses, and people lacking EQ struggle to cope with that stress.

Block Mistakes: People with lower EQs often get stuck on their mistakes and refuse to look further, or forget about them, condemning them to repeat the same mistakes again. Feeling Misunderstood: People with lower EQs can't convey their emotions clearly because they don't understand them on their own, leaving ample room for misinterpretation.

Lack of understanding what your emotional triggers are: Everyone has some sort of trigger, something that immediately provokes intense and often irrational responses to some kind of stimulus. Those who lack EQ often don't know what theirs are.

Hiding Emotions: People with lower EQs tend to see negative emotions poorly and prefer to keep them hidden behind positive ones instead. This means that their needs are never addressed because they never use their negative emotions.

Blaming Others For How They Make You Feel: People with lower EQs hold other people accountable for triggering their emotional responses instead of acknowledging that no one is responsible for their emotional states.

Being easily offended: Those with a lower EQ typically lack the self-confidence of those with a higher EQ. They also require an understanding of their strengths and weaknesses, which makes them a little more self-conscious when called upon.

Self-management

Self-management involves the ability to dictate one's thoughts, feelings and behaviours. This emotional intelligence quadrant focuses on your ability to manage yourself. It includes your responses to those around you and the situations you might find yourself in, as well as expressing your positive emotions as you control adverse reactions. While it's acceptable to have negative emotions, they should never be in control of you as a person. You should be able to handle negative feelings without harming others or letting yourself go wild. It involves using self-awareness to keep those negative feelings in your control, as you can identify what they are and why you feel them.

Some of the abilities frequently encountered in people with high self-management include:

Maintaining control of emotions: the ability to recognize and feel emotions without letting them dictate behaviour.

Reliable: These people are trustworthy and are often committed to accomplishing what they have agreed to do.

Flexible: the ability to proceed with change when it comes unexpectedly without ruining plans or preventing the individual from achieving other goals.

Optimistic: Negative feelings are not enough to discourage him from trying to achieve the desired results.

You are motivated to Achieve Goals: Knowing what you want and driven to make it happen.

Willing to take the initiative: at ease being the one who initiates the change e

Low self-management

Struggle to Control Emotions: People with low self-management struggle to keep their feelings, and therefore their actions, in check. They typically respond emotionally rather than rationally.

 Struggle to accept criticism: Anything negative said to those with low self-management struggle to keep disappointment or other negative emotions in check after feeling criticized.

Unable to cope with change or the unexpected: Those with lower self-management struggle when things don't go according to plan. Dealing with change is difficult, as change or the unexpected usually goes hand in hand with stronger negative emotions.

Impulsive: Those with low self-management struggle to keep their impulses in check. When they get the chance, they'll take something they like best, even if it has worse consequences. The consequence is not as necessary as the happiness of getting along with the impulse.

You Need Instant Gratification: Often, people with less self-management tend to go with gratification sooner rather than waiting for a better outcome. For example, they are likely to buy something they cannot afford in cash and put it on a credit card where they will pay significant amounts of interest if the alternative has been waiting for months to be able to afford to pay in cash. They prefer to have the item first, even if the consequences are worse.

Social awareness

Social awareness focuses on understanding what other people want and need. It is the ability to look at someone else and know how they are feeling or what they need at that particular moment. Those who are socially aware can tell at a glance how they should approach another person and how to stay calm in situations. They often go out of their way to meet other people's needs just because they feel they can, so they should. They often exhibit some of these traits:

Empath: A deep understanding of how someone else is feeling and what is needed right now.

An understanding of group structures: they recognize how society works and the community idea of giving and take where everyone contributes something.

Service-Oriented: They prioritize other people's needs and wants to ensure they are met as much as possible.

When you have a high level of social awareness, you can consider the wants and needs of others adequately and satisfy them quickly. These people often excel at being leaders or public speakers - they excel at speaking the way people want to hear, and they use that skill to get the support they need in their work. These people are typically quite charismatic, but also selfless in the sense that they are doing their best to ensure that the needs of others are taken into consideration. Social awareness requires a developed sense of self-awareness to be genuinely useful.

Low social awareness

Unconfident: Those who have no social awareness typically do not trust those around them, nor do they earn the trust of those around them.

Never satisfying the needs of others, they never assert themselves as trustworthy.

Lack of empathy: When social awareness is lacking, it is quite challenging to understand what others are feeling. They struggle to relate meaningfully to other people because they fail to understand the needs of others entirely.

 Selfish: When social awareness and empathy don't play a role in life, people don't feel the pressure to ensure that others' needs are met.

Manipulators: Those who don't have much social awareness don't feel uncomfortable using other people to get what they want. Their lack of empathy means they don't care so much about hurting other people.

Closed Mindset: Social awareness allows for thoughts of diversity and an understanding of how each person, no matter how different, can contribute in some way. Those who lack common knowledge may not see the use of some people's skills or understand how nonessential jobs or skills can still contribute to the overall well-being of society. Isolated: Because those who lack social awareness do not trust others and lack sophisticated empathy, they typically retire on their own rather than associate with other people.

They do not create social support groups and instead live alone.

Relationship management

Relationship management is the most complex of the four quadrants of emotional intelligence. It involves the ability to influence other people through your own words and actions, allowing for inspiration and the ability to mediate and resolve conflicts that may arise within the groups you are inspiring. This is the crucial trait for leaders - it's what allows you to lead expertly and kindly, earning that position instead of having to take it through domination. Those with high relationship management skills make informed decisions about their interactions with others so that they can achieve the desired outcome that best suits the needs at the time.

1. Decide on how best to proceed in the current situation. You have taken the time to analyze how people around you feel and to identify the reasons for those feelings. From there, you will decide what the most effective ways to interact with those around you, as well as consider the potential reactions you might get based on how you approach them are. You will also discuss how their results will affect you and have

plans and skills in place to manage those potentially negative feelings effectively and appropriately.

2. Interact with others the way you have determined is the best course of action possible. These interactions can vary in form. For example, it could be written or verbal and with a single person or the whole group.

3. Identify a result you want and adapt your interactions to that result. You will interact with people in ways you know will influence them to create the outcome you want, adding an intentional element to the act of relationship management.

4. Identify needs you are trying to meet to make sure the result is right for the situation. You want your outcome to meet the needs of yourself, the people around you, or whatever needs your decision is addressing at that particular moment.

People with high relationship management skills typically exhibit the following traits:

- Influential

- Inspirational

- Invested in the development of other people

- Willing to be the catalyst for change

- Acting as a mediator of the conflict

- Cultivate and encourage bonds between people within the group

- Create teams that work well together and promote teamwork or collaboration

Low relationship management

Ineffective leader: Those who struggle with relationship management fail to fill leadership roles. They are typically too self-centred or socially blind to understand the nuances behind leading a group effectively

Untrustworthy and unwelcome: Typically, those with poor relationship management struggle to be trustworthy or likeable.People prefer to avoid them.

Act selfishly: They may not recognize the needs of others, or simply don't care about others' needs for other reasons. Regardless, they don't inspire much loyalty when they refuse to help others. They're not exciting: No matter how much they ask other people to help them or do something, people don't feel motivated, obligated, or eager to do what was asked.

They likely see a constant revolving door of new **employees or relationships:** As these people struggle with relationships, they often see new ones, both at work and in their personal life. This constant updating of people in a person's life means they never truly learn how to develop meaningful relationships.

The interrelation of Emotional Components of intelligence.

Within emotional intelligence, all four quadrants are interrelated. They build on each other to create a well-rounded and emotionally intelligent individual. The necessary foundation is self-awareness; having some degree of self-awareness gives you a chance to start thinking about both self-management and social awareness. If you struggle with self-awareness, you are likely to have a hard time moving on to the next stage of self-management or social recognition. Often, self-awareness is one of the best places to start practising and strengthening one's emotional intelligence, as others require skills developed through self-awareness to be active with others.

After self-awareness has been developed, self-management and social awareness become possible. You cannot manage yourself and your emotions if you lack a basic understanding of what your feelings are or how they work, and similarly, if you are not aware of your beliefs, you cannot hope to understand how someone is feeling—other or what you might need. The development of both self-management and social awareness leads to the ability to start developing relationship management. Without self-awareness, the whole process of developing emotional intelligence becomes increasingly tricky. It takes a mastery of self-awareness, self-management and social awareness to start learning relationship management.

Effects of EI on your relationships and your work

You can't eliminate the need to interact with other people. Even if you do, you still have to fight yourself! Instead of trying to avoid people, your most viable option is first to learn to manage yourself and then to manage those around you, especially those with whom you spend the most time at home, at work, or school. Whether you tend to react negatively to yourself and others or you tend to get overwhelmed with positive emotions and push your boundaries, both are signs that you need to work on your emotional intelligence.

Impact of EI on your relationships

Genuinely connecting with what others feel is a function of empathy. With this skill, you build stronger bonds with your partner, friends and family. You don't necessarily have to solve other people's problems for them to feel a strong affinity with you. Everyone wants to be understood, and empathy is one of the best ways to show others that you know them. When you appreciate where others are coming from, it's easier not to judge them harshly.

Conversations don't get out of hand quickly in a relationship where one or both partners are willing to put themselves in the other's shoes. In other words, instead of turning off due to criticism, you can see the pure intent behind the feedback even if it was poorly provided—your ability to take criticism without arguing shows that you are willing to learn and improve.

In intimate relationships, emotional intelligence helps you not be afraid of being vulnerable. Being vulnerable is a difficult thing for many people. Still, your ability to recognize what prevents you from completely letting your guard down with someone you love is a display of emotional intelligence.

Vulnerability is not a display of weakness; it takes a tremendous amount of strength and character to be vulnerable. However, knowing exactly when and with whom to be vulnerable requires a high level of emotional intelligence.

People who are not assertive can suppress their true feelings and use passive aggression to communicate disapproval. Not being able to express an unmet emotional need, especially in intimate relationships, can lead to a breakdown in communication. But emotionally intelligent people can say exactly what they want and don't want without being aggressive.

More importantly, emotional intelligence can quickly make you apologize when you are wrong. Holding a grudge or finding it hard to apologize when you are wrong is a sign of low emotional intelligence. Conflicts are bound to arise in relationships - there are no two ways to do this. However, putting your need for intimacy with your partner above the need to be right can make you ask for amends during conflicts.

Impact of EI on your work

There is no pause button for your emotions. You take them wherever you go, including your workplace. You hear them interacting with employees and co-workers, which is why emotions can make the difference between a great career and a poor one or an outstanding entrepreneur/leader and one who doesn't get along with others.

In addition to possessing a high IQ, high emotional intelligence is required to be successful at work. People with high emotional intelligence tend to solve problems better and are generally better at making decisions. This is because they are more socially aware and can evaluate situations against the bigger picture. Even when under the pressure of deadlines, impossible bosses and annoying colleagues, they don't quickly lose their temper. And because they have a healthy dose of empathy, they can quickly build a strong relationship with others. A high level of emotional intelligence in the workplace can prevent conflicts from escalating. Those who work to improve their emotional intelligence are also open to listening and reflecting on positive and negative feedback.

More, people with low emotional intelligence are challenging to team up at work because they lack empathy and social skills. They are usually not open to the opinions of others and can become aggressive in their communication or display a passive communication style. They would rather play the role of a victim or shift the blame instead of taking personal responsibility for the mistakes.

Despite your current level of emotional intelligence, it can be polished and refined. All it takes is a continuous practice. And as long as you are alive, there are plenty of opportunities to practice your emotional intelligence skills every day.

<u>**Chapter 6**</u>
The Importance of Empathy

There is a vast difference between empathy and pity. Insight is compassion for others. It is walking in the shoes of others to understand how they feel. This can help you know the most appropriate approach to take in dealing with them. Piety, on the other hand, is looking at other people from a perspective that has no power. To feel compassion for someone is to assume that they are unable to do anything about their situation and that they need you to be their saviour. Having compassion for people doesn't help them. Instead, it keeps them in a place of addiction and ultimately drains you of your emotional energy. It is vital to know this difference so that as you connect with others, you can be attentive to codependent relationships and empowering relationships.

Working to improve your level of empathy doesn't keep you wandering around looking for someone to have mercy on. Instead, you attract people who sincerely seek to be lifted and pushed into their path to you. You don't need to worry if you think your empathy level is low. Empathy can be improved with the right practices. Let's take glance at how to do it.

Empathy: the secret to connecting with others

Empathy is classified into affective, cognitive, and compassionate understanding. Understanding these categories of compassion can help you channel your energy in the right direction.

1. Affective empathy: refers to the ability to connect deeply and share the feelings of others. It is being able to feel the emotions of others as if you were physically having the same experience with them. It is useful for building strong interpersonal relationships and a healthy relationship. But it has a very debilitating drawback. It can prevent you from seeing the bigger picture and leads to decisions based on current impulses. Decisive choices that would be for the greater good are hardly reached when one is stuck in affective empathy. If you are in a situation of leadership, this kind of level of understanding can negatively impact your ability to lead effectively.

2. Cognitive empathy: this is the intellectual aspect of compassion. It is a clear understanding of the perspectives of others without necessarily sharing their feelings. It helps you get inside the other person's head to get to know their point of view. Doctors, for example, can understand their patients' feelings without necessarily sharing them. You can effectively negotiate with others to your advantage if you get inside their heads without necessarily sharing their opinions. However, this type of empathy prevents you from experiencing the deep feelings of others. Your connection with them is superficial, as is your relationship with them. To truly connect with others without getting lost in their emotions requires a different kind of empathy: compassionate empathy.

3. Compassionate empathy: as you have rightly guessed, this is the middle point between the type of affective and cognitive empathy. It is, in fact, a combination of an intellectual understanding of the situation of others and how exactly they feel. In other words, you are in their head and heart to determine the most appropriate response and action to take if necessary. You have no compassion for people, nor are you cold towards them. You do not have a predefined answer to all situations. Instead, you evaluate each case based on its peculiarities and manage them consciously. Compassionate empathy helps you keep your focus on what's right and right in your attempt to help others. You don't jeopardize the right thing just to please others, nor are you firmly attached to the rules when you have to be human.

Develop empathy

Okay, so how does the right amount of strong empathy develop? How do you balance affective and cognitive empathy so that you don't get fooled and don't appear unfriendly? Well, it doesn't happen overnight. The key is to take baby steps as you practice the following tips.

1. Face your emotions first: You don't have much to offer others to help them overcome emotional challenges if you are not responsible for your feelings. So, your first sequence of business is to make sure you understand your psychological processes and how to deal with them.

2. To observe: When interacting with people, notice how you feel about what they say and do. What emotion does their behaviour evoke in you as you listen to them or observe their action? Take control of yourself by psychologically distancing yourself from the feeling so that you don't get overwhelmed and react immediately to the emotion. This will give you time to process their behaviour and emotional response.

3. Focus on the problems: Instead of being blown away by the emotions the other person is feeling, try first to determine what is causing those emotions. Keeping your focus on real problems will help you maintain rational thinking and the right perspective during interactions.

4. Practice active listening: Wait a while to offer advice and solutions when people share their problems with you. When you tell someone what they should or shouldn't have done immediately after sharing a problem with you, it invalidates their experience. Instead, say something that shows that you understand where they come from and how they feel. For example, "I may not be in your shoes right now, and I can't even understand how you feel, but I can see how hard it is for you ..." Something like this will make the other person open and available to listen to yours. Tips. Practising active listening is a compelling balance between affective and cognitive empathy.

5. Apologize only if necessary: Don't allow yourself to feel sorry about something that is not entirely your fault or that has nothing to do with you. Don't let your feelings to cloud your thought process.

While it's a good thing to apologize when you're wrong and take responsibility for your mistakes, make sure you don't respond to others' blame pattern. An excessive apology does not make you socially likeable, nor does it help build stronger relationships. Instead, it shows a lack of self-confidence and is polite behaviour for people.

6. Be authentic: Let your body language convey the same message as your words. You will be seen as trustworthy and will only attract others when your verbal and non-verbal expressions are congruent. Showing empathy doesn't mean pretending. Don't say what you don't mean just to please others.

7. Practice: Look for opportunities to show empathy because this is how you can improve. It doesn't matter if you end up leaning too much on the cognitive or emotional side. What matters is that you go out into the real world and practice what you read. Over time, you will become better at showing appropriate levels of empathy.

Detection and management of energy vampires

Simply put, an energy vampire is someone who drains your emotional energy, intentionally or unknowingly.

They could be your closest friend, a distant relative, or even a particular situation (such as certain TV shows, public locations, and so on). If you feel overwhelmed, exhausted, stressed, or guilty every time you interact with someone, they may unduly take advantage of your empathy and use it against you. It is also a clear indication that you need to work to improve your level of understanding because you may be relying too much on affective empathy.

To help you deal with these toxic people, you need to develop both self-awareness and social awareness. Self-awareness will warn you of your feelings when you are in contact with these people, and social awareness will help you avoid them without causing conflict. You will learn more about how to use these tools in later chapters, but for now, let's focus on how to identify and manage energy vampires.

Energy vampire signs

Energy vampires come in different types ranging from martyr or victim vampire to narcissistic vampire and everyone else in between. But I won't bother you with this information. Instead, I'd like you to focus on identifying energy vampires in general so that you can recognize and relate to them appropriately. Here are some signs to help you realize energy vampires.

They try to show you how insignificant your problems are compared to theirs. For example, "I know your job is demanding, but at least you have a job!"

They use guilt as a tool to manipulate others to get what they want. For example, "You'll do it for me if you love me."

They always blame others. They are never guilty of anything going wrong, but they want to take all the credit when things go well.

They are usually involved in one type of drama or another and expect you to be their saviour! For example, "Everyone keeps picking on me for no reason. You're the only person left I can trust."

They always want to outshine or outdo others even when there is no basis for competition. They do this because they find it challenging to feel truly happy for others. For example, "Congratulations, I'm so happy for you! You just have to work a little harder to get to where I am."

They always behave in a way that calls attention to their acts of self-pity. They complain, complain and put on a show as if they were respectful martyrs. All this in an attempt to garner emotional support for their declining self-esteem. For example, "Regardless of everything I do and have been through for him, he's still ungrateful."

They take unfair advantage of the good nature of others. If they observe that you are kindhearted, sensitive to the situation of others and looking for the good in others, they can take advantage of it to ask for infinite favours because you will not want to hurt them by saying no.

Dealing with energy vampires

Allowing people to continue draining your energy can have very adverse effects on you. Low energy levels for a long time can lead to anxiety, depression, and other stress-related physical and mental illnesses. If you have identified an energy vampire, relate to them with the following in mind to avoid getting sucked into their emotional black hole.

1. Maintain brief eye contact. The eyes have rightly been described as the window to the soul. The longer you maintain eye contact with an energy vampire, the more direct access it has to your energy reserves. Eye contact can keep you busy with them and deplete your energy levels faster.

2. Establish and enforce healthy boundaries. Be steadfast when you don't like something and never back down. Otherwise, you will send mixed signals. Limit your interactions with them as much as possible.

3. Avoid pushing them against. If you feel the urge to contradict or argue with an energy vampire, move away from him if possible or close him mentally. Involving them in topics or trying to change their points of view is an effort in the wrong direction. You can't change anyone unless they're willing to. Pushing against them will leave you drained.

4. Save your energy if you have to carry on a conversation with them. In other words, listen more than you talk. Limit your words and ask short questions such as how, when and why you will keep them talking for the most part and conserve your energy. In essence, you are doing them a world of good because many well-meaning energy vampires are merely looking for someone to listen to them.

5. Set a time limit beyond which you will not go for an energy vampire. You don't want to spend time with someone who can leave you insane. If you feel that 10 minutes of your time is all you can give a person, don't exceed that time limit.

6. Break contact with an energy vampire that you have identified as harmful to your emotional and physical health. Some emotional vampires are easy to deal with, especially if they have no intentional intentions of hurting you. But when a person is intent on dragging you to their toxic level, stop all contact with them. It can be a difficult decision, but your happiness is more important than maintaining an unhealthy relationship.

Empathy for energy vampires

Resenting or hating someone secretly can also drain your emotional energy. So, while trying to avoid energy vampires, you can inadvertently deprive yourself of your energy by becoming resentful. Recognize that some people don't intend to hurt you or drain your energy. They simply haven't learned to manage their powers properly. Sometimes, these people sincerely seek help or cry out for an unmet emotional need: validation, love, attention, and affection. As you set boundaries, be kind to them too. Dealing with energy vampires will require more cognitive empathy than affective empathy. In other words, you'll need to better connect with them on an intellectual level to understand their point of view without being emotionally drawn to how they feel.

Chapter 7

Improving Your Social Skills And Relationships

Your efforts to read and learn about emotional intelligence won't have any significant impact on you if you fail to combine self-awareness with empathy to improve you relate to others. After all, your relationship doesn't begin and end with yourself. As I said earlier, there is no shortage of opportunities to practice the various aspects of emotional intelligence. Examples of opportunities where emotional intelligence comes into play include:

Provide critical feedback to your friend, child, spouse, or employee.

You are taming your urge to overspend because you're in a good mood.

You are deciding between two equally talented people or situations to pay your attention when they both need your attention at the same time.

Show compassion to an employee or co-worker when their problems impact job performance.

They are helping your teen or subordinate child find a balance between being more responsible for their actions and empowering them through delegation.

Decide which investments are worth.

Strengthen your child's confidence when he feels excluded from his peers.

You are dealing with an angry customer or a customer who is yelling at you for something that isn't entirely your fault.

To console someone who has suffered a considerable loss.

Pacify a child who throws a tantrum.

In these and similar situations, a hands-on demonstration of social skills is needed to prevent the situation from escalating and your relationship to precipitate. Developing your social skills will automatically result in lasting relationships. But you cannot effectively build your social skills without first reaching a certain level of self-awareness and having a firm grip on yourself through self-management. Let's take a closer look at some practical steps to improve these two aspects: self-awareness and self-management.

Become more self-aware

The phrase "Know thyself" is not just a fanciful old inscription on the walls of the temple of Apollo in ancient Greece. It is relevant now as it was the first time Socrates uttered it. If you are to develop self-awareness, you must be ready to face your demons. Some of the things you'll discover about yourself may not be pleasant, but the process is necessary if you want to master your weaknesses. Likewise, you also need to recognize your strengths. Don't ignore or minimize your muscles and put the spotlight only on your real or perceived inadequacies. Self-awareness, used in this book, is a tool that helps you embrace yourself as you are and recognize what you need to do to have better relationships.

Here are some clear-cut methods you can use to become more self-aware.

1. Keep a record of your emotions, especially the ones you felt before you decided to say or behave in a certain way you didn't like. Also, write down what triggered the emotion: was it someone or a particular situation? How did you feel about the location or the person's words or behaviour? Try to think back to when you have felt this way in the past. Was the

situation similar or was the same person involved? Your goal in this step is to find a pattern and not just isolated events. A trigger pattern will give you the right information to understand how emotion is triggered in you. This is the first step towards self-regulation.

2. You can notice how people react to your behaviour. Set aside a couple of minutes each day, for example, in the evenings, then try to remember how people responded to something you did or said. What trend is the general reaction - positive or negative? Review the responses honestly to see if you need to make corrections in your behaviour.

3. Another thing I highly recommend you do is to interrupt your day and reconnect with your emotions. It's easy to get carried away with daily activities by losing touch with your feelings. When you are not aware of what your emotions are signalling, you can behave in ways that you will regret later on. To minimize, set reminders on your mobile device, alarm clock or laptop. Alternatively, mentally associate your interrupt with a trigger like the sound of a siren, the sound of a clock at the start of the hour, or something that occurs fairly regularly. Whenever your alarm goes

off, or the interruption goes off, take a couple of minutes to reflect on how you feel right now and in the last few minutes. If you continue this practice several times a day, it will soon become a habit, and you no longer need a reminder or trigger to reconnect with your emotions. If you can listen to what your feelings tell you several times a day, you will significantly reduce hasty reactions.

4. You can also ask for honest feedback from those close to you. It doesn't matter if they are your friends and family or not, as long as you spend a significant amount of time with them directly or indirectly, they can give you feedback on your behaviours. But don't do this if you expect to get watered down opinions. It takes a high level of courage and sincerity to face this challenge. To get others to evaluate you without bias, ask them to give you the feedback anonymously. Please note, however, that not all input is correct. If someone says something about you that you know is incorrect, at least you know what they think about your behaviour. On the other hand, if something they said about you is correct even though it might be painful, it gives you a chance to make changes.

5. One final method I would suggest to improve your self-awareness is to name your emotions. To do this:

When you start to feel an emotion welling up inside you, deliberately stop talking or taking any action. Just stop.

Take a few breaths and try to identify and name the emotion. It doesn't have to be an accurate description of the excitement. For example, fear can be described as doubt, worry, nervousness, and so on.

Simply observe the emotions you have identified without judgment. Now, tell yourself it's okay to feel that way, but remind yourself that you don't have to act on the emotion, at least not immediately.

Here is an example. You may feel worried about a bogus meeting with your picky boss. Take a mental break and take a few deep breaths. Say something like: "At the moment I am feeling anxious and a little nervous about this meeting. It is okay that I think this way, but the result I fear may or may not happen. I will wait to be more rational before taking any action. "

This exercise helps you develop metacognition, the identification of your cognitive processes. It helps you take charge of your emotions in the early stages before they get out of your conscious control. As you continue to practice this, you will gain the ability to become the impartial observer of your experiences instead of being so absorbed in your skills that you become oblivious to your internal cues and their meanings.

Because self-awareness is important

So, what exactly do you get by being more self-aware? First, being self-aware removes the unproductive process of beating yourself up for your mistakes. Instead, channel your energy to learn from mistakes. Being self-aware means knowing your emotional limits, so you don't get caught off guard by people or situations. It helps you look for people who can complement you in areas of your weakness. This is especially useful if you work in a team. Furthermore, you are aware of your choices as you are not easily overwhelmed by waves of emotions. You can also capitalize on your identified strengths to help you reach your goals faster instead of wasting time on goals that aren't in line with your muscles.

Self-management

Recognizing your emotions and even naming them is one thing, controlling yourself not to act on a whim is another no-brainer. While identifying your emotions can slow down your reaction process, it doesn't automatically eliminate the feeling. Self-management skills are needed to provide alternative outlets to release your emotions to avoid buildup and uncontrollable outbursts.

When you master self-management skills, you can stay focused on your goals and tasks regardless of the emotions you feel. You will be able to determine when and how much excitement is suitable for different situations. In other words, you can control and direct your choices, even in emotional situations.

Self-management is not to be confused with the selective numbing of certain emotions. You can't go through life, always feeling positive emotions. It wouldn't be a healthy way to live. Both pleasant and stimulating feelings serve essential purposes and should not be neglected at all. The use of learning how to improve your self-management skills is to gain control over your reactions to emotions and not suffocate them.

To improve your self-management skills, I invite you to apply the following methods.

1. Mentally move away from the trigger. If you can do it physically too, it will be worth it. The more distance you create between yourself and the stressful situation, the calmer you will become and the more comfortable you will regain control of your thought process. Practice breathing deeply as you move away (mentally and physically) from the situation. This is an effective way to stay calm under pressure.

2. Learn to listen more during stressful situations. Instead of arguing and arguing, allow the other person who may be feeling irritable to say what is on their mind without interrupting them.

Rephrase their words as you understand them to see if you are both on the same page before deciding what an appropriate answer would be.

3. Don't blame your mistakes. Don't get defensive and argue about your limits. Your best defence is to accept responsibility for any errors on your part and take steps to correct them.

4. Think about the possible impact of your actions before responding. When you take short breaks before acting or speaking, try to imagine what the consequences of your reaction would be. If you have already reacted in this way, what was the result? Would you like a repeat of that result? If not, it would be better to consider other ways to respond.

5. Be open to change. Fighting change almost certainly leads to injury. If a process or opinion is different than what you know, temporarily suspend your disbelief and see if there might be something helpful in the seemingly opposite view. That way, you stay true to your values while being open to new ideas.

Here are some other exercises that can also improve your self-management skills.

No matter how busy you are, make time for laughter and fun every day.

Maintain a healthy work-life balance. Allowing the two to overlap can lead to unnecessary stress.

Give yourself enough time (7 to 8 hours) to get a good night's sleep.

Consider including mindfulness practices, meditation, alone time, or controlled breathing as part of your daily activities. These practices can also improve your self-awareness as they give you space to reflect on yourself.

Get at least thirty minutes of daily movement.

If you drink alcohol, try drinking water or reducing your alcohol usage drastically.

Why is self-management so important?

Behaving intelligently is not achieved by happenstance. It demands constant practice in self-management skills. This is one of the advantages of training to enhance your self-management skills. You will be able to think before behaving or responding to persons or situations. Regrets for inappropriate behaviors, inactions, and expressions are greatly decreased as a result of self-regulation. Instead of being reactive, you may become proactive in your behavioral reactions.

Chapter 8: Emotional Management

<u>Recognizing your emotions</u>
<u>It is fairly unusual for people to believe that negative feelings are fundamentally negative and imply that a person is wrong. It's natural to want to feel happy most of the time, but it doesn't mean you should feel bad about how you think. Don't think you're wrong because you're feeling bad, or that someone else is better than you because they're feeling wonderful. Feelings are what they are, and you cannot and should not control how you think. Allow feelings to do what they were created to do: communicate information to you. Your task is to concentrate on how to regulate your reactions to how you feel. To put it another way,</u>

<u>In other words, your perspective of the environment (whether positive or negative) impacts which signals get released in your body. Your emotions reflect your perception or comprehension of the events going on around you. Although not all emotions are the same, they are generally neutral. In other words, they are neither good nor harmful. Some people may feel wonderful,</u>

while others may feel horrible, but feelings are crucial indicators that tell you whether to continue forward or approach with caution. Do you see how concealing a feeling is counterproductive? Instead of suppressing an emotion, pay attention to its message and select your

response.

Each emotion is associated with a message. However, if you haven't practiced listening to it, you will miss the word. Here are four examples:

and messages. Study them to get an idea of what your emotions are telling you. The words may vary depending on the individual and their core beliefs, but the chart gives you a general idea of what each emotion represents.

Gaining control over your emotions

So what t do you feel bad and shouldn't be suppressing your emotions? First of all, understand that suppressing your emotions is not true self-regulation or management. Even if your intentions are good, suppressing your feelings can lead to resentment in relationships, insincerity, more negative feelings, and high blood pressure if you keep doing it for a long time.

However, expressing or acting on your emotions the way you feel them can be disastrous. The goal of improving your emotional intelligence will be defeated if you keep working on your feelings because you don't want to suppress them. Your best approach would be to reevaluate your emotions.

Reevaluating your emotions means seeking alternative interpretations for a problematic situation. Right self-management involves accepting changes. If something goes against your beliefs, your feelings will trigger an emotional response in you to alert you to the contradiction. But if you expand your vision to include new ideas, your emotions will transform according to the new set of beliefs. This is why you need to be willing to look at things from other perspectives while staying true to your core values.

To effectively reevaluate a situation, you must necessarily suspend your disbelief. For example, your partner hasn't kept their promise, and you feel terrible. Fighting with them will not make them feel good, nor will it change the situation. On the other hand, ignoring how you feel and wearing a soft smile doesn't improve your mood either. When you reevaluate the case, you will start thinking along the lines of:

"They may have failed me, but I'm sure they aren't failures themselves."

"I cannot force them to do what they are not willing to do. Maybe I expect too much of them. "

"Maybe they didn't mean to hurt me or not keep their promises. I too, have made mistakes in the past."

Thinking this way will broaden your horizons and allow you to embrace other possibilities. With this understanding will come relief from negative emotions you may have experienced previously. And in that free space, you're in a better place to make the right decisions that you won't regret later on.

Here are two quick, simple, but effective exercises to help you manage your emotions.

1. When you find yourself in a situation where your emotions run wild, deliberately reduce your heart rate by shortening the inhalations and prolonging the exhalations. This will effectively reduce blood pressure and the urge to react immediately.

2. Think of the situation as a challenge rather than a threat. Facing a problem is more motivating than facing a threat. Usually, you will avoid danger but look for ways to overcome a challenge.

It is essential always to remember that it is not necessary to rush to react if there is no immediate danger. If you can keep your emotions in check, you will be able to handle situations rationally no matter how difficult they may seem at first.

Chapter 9

Learn To Lead And Why Emotionally Intelligent People Are The Best Leaders

The self-awareness and problem-solving skills found in people considered emotionally intelligent make them impeccable leaders. Emotionally smart people are often the ones who don't mind stepping up and volunteering to take responsibility. A leader is someone who takes responsibility and can be trusted to guide his followers in the right direction. Psychologists today can agree that we need more leaders in the world, which is why the curriculum in schools that promotes emotional intelligence is so relevant. Below we will discuss how to become a leader and why these traits make a person better suited to lead.

Leaders are team players. Teamwork is vital not only for the quality of your work but, in the most extreme cases, for survival. Building a team takes advantage of everyone's collective talents and helps you complete projects promptly, so when you work on aside, a good team player knows their strengths and weaknesses.

They have something to bring to the table. It is more than likely that you are looking to build a team because it will take more than one person to deal with this problem, so do your best to use your strengths. Get involved and let your teammates know that you are great at something, and most importantly, show up and commit.

Secondly, you should be able to drive from any position. You may not have an official title or be the head of the company, but that doesn't stop you from being able to step up and lead when a leader is needed. Taking on a difficult task or improving your workplace is a quick way to get noticed by your employer. Show that you have some courage. Someday it will be time for your supervisor to leave his position and you will most likely be the first person you can think of to replace him. You don't need to be formally instructed to step up and take control when change is required.

We've already discussed in this book how being an expert on some skills helps you be an emotionally smarter person, but you should also know that it's okay that you don't know everything, just try to make sure you know something. Let's assume you are doing very well at what you already do. That is great! But you should try to learn new skills that apply to the new things your job requires. Don't just lean back and accept that "it's not my job; I won't do it". Go beyond your abilities, even in everyday life, not just in the workplace.

As a leader, you be open and accept criticism. One trait that EVERYONE hates in a leader is not able to take that they are sometimes wrong. They refuse to admit that they are wrong and often end up blaming someone else. Use this criticism to become a better person. Use it to grow as a leader. No leader will be perfect in the beginning, and receiving criticism should flatter you. When your followers feel comfortable enough talking to you to give you blame, you know you've done an excellent job communicating.

Use every opportunity you can get your hands on to communicate with your team and ask them what they need. You should be able to show that you understand what is required of you as your team leader and that you understand your team's limitations. Always strive to improve the quality and efficiency of your work, but avoid becoming overbearing. All it takes sometimes is an early workday meeting with some sort of open mic feel. Let the team express what they want from this project and what they need to do their best job and, if reasonable, provide that kind of environment for them.

This brings us to communication skills. Good leaders can communicate effectively and clearly with their teams. This includes proper email formatting and professional writing and speaking. Be consistent in what you say and don't extend the truth for any reason. You should be honest with your team because you would expect them to be honest with you. Avoid becoming emotionally with them and keep your tone appropriate. It's encouraging for your team to have a harsh attitude when you have one first. They are a mirror reflection of what you are projecting onto them.

Also, eliminate your desires from the actions you take for the team. Being a good leader requires sacrifices, and the best thing for the team may not be the best thing for you. Loyalty is a rare trait and displays excellent character. In the corporate environment, reliability is as outstanding as showing up for work. Don't make recommendations that conflict with what's happening and give credit for the finished project to your team, not yourself. When your unit starts believing that your motivations are suitable for everyone and not just yourself, they begin to like you and trust you.

Encourage creativity within your team. Letting your team know that they can express themselves allows them to feel comfortable doing their best work. Enough time should be left to feel comfortable while working on the side because feeling uncomfortable will make things worse for everyone. Intellectually stimulate your team members and encourage them to think. Ask questions and expect answers. Offering a challenge to your group will provide the stimulus they need to feel comfortable and interested, and a challenging task makes it fun.

Overall, be a passionate and expressive role model for your team. You should present a version of yourself who is the kind of leader your team members want to be. Be a role model for the qualities you want to see in your teammates. You will find that they will be better suited to start mirroring your actions. After all, your followers are a reflection of who you are, and that's a big responsibility! Show them what the model looks like and they will. Keep that kind of integrity close because it's valuable and smart to have.

Chapter 10
Starting to Practice Empathy

Empathy is putting yourself in the place of others. Emotionally intelligent people use awareness of their emotions to stop toxic behaviours first and consider how others are feeling. You can always improve your empathy. Empathy helps heal relationships and create new ones. Being a sensitive person doesn't make you weak or some kind of second-hand person. It gives you an idea of the feelings of others and increases your awareness of the emotional atmosphere around you. Here are some ways you can learn to practice empathy better and grow as an emotionally intelligent person.

Studies show that empathy is only partially an innate behaviour, and it is partly learned. Facing challenges and learning your limits can help humiliate you. Humility makes it easier for you to feel what people feel when they feel like a failure, and humility erases the cheekiness and annoying behaviours you might once have had. By staying active and avoiding unwanted behaviours, you will be positioned around emotions more frequently, which opens a window to opportunities. The emotional growth you get by doing new things and pushing yourself is worth the frustration.

Go out of the home. Live your life a little. You should try to get out of your comfort zone. Seeing the world and other cultures helps you appreciate them better. It helps you to appreciate diversity better. Empathy comes from enjoying someone else's feelings and being able to understand why they feel that way. Their experience in life was probably different from yours, and they may have learned to react differently to that type of situation than you do. We all need to collectively understand that we all feel differently and are entitled to our feelings.

Ask your friends and family what they think about your empathy skills. Ask them to answer honestly and let you know if you have been too soft or too hard in the past. Remember, we're not afraid of criticism here and will take it humbly. Criticism is nothing more than an opportunity to improve. In particular, ask your peers what they think about your relationship skills. If they let you know that you could improve something, make an effort to improve and ask them again periodically if they can see a difference.

Educating yourself should never be embarrassing; it should be a comfortable and positive experience.

Listen to what your telling you and not so much your head. You may be quick to judge when you see someone cry over an experience that you feel you have personally handled well, but as far as you know, they may have gone through a lot more than you are seeing. Maybe even recently they lost their jobs or went through a bad breakup. Don't judge your books by their cover; put yourself in their place instead. Think about how they feel more than you think about them at the moment. When your brain tells you to let someone else deal, hopefully, your heart is asking you to take some time out of your day to comfort that person who needs your help. You could very well save their lives.

When you talk to others about their problems, ask them what their situation is like. Try to see things from their perspective so you can get all the details before you start making hypotheses. Ask them how they perceive you and listen. They should feel comfortable opening you up to these things, so if they feel uncomfortable, don't overdo it. Anything they disclose should be confidential and consenting. When you finally see things on their side, you may be surprised at how similar their situation may seem to something you have experienced. Getting to know their job better will help you help them.

Perhaps you should also take a moment to examine your prejudices. Everyone has things that cause them to think or react in a certain way, but it helps us become more emotionally aware of ourselves when we can catch ourselves red-handed and instead say no. It is best for the emotionally intelligent person to make choices based on all the information they have and to ignore the biases we know we have. This leads to better decision making and a fairer view. It doesn't make you a wrong person for having prejudices, as many of them stem from influences you first noticed when you were very young, but it makes you a better person to be able to put them aside for the sake of rationality.

Empathy works best even when you are a good listener. Listening to someone makes them feel more comfortable trusting you with their concerns and makes them feel important. You will also learn from them. Some of us only listen to half as much as we speak, but we just take the time to keep quiet.

Becoming a more empathic listener involves giving the conversation your undivided attention, giving the speaker plenty of chances to get it all out and say what he needs to say, ask insightful questions, and summarize what you heard after you finish speaking.

Once you realize that you are more able to empathize with your peers, you will find yourself becoming more aware of your prejudices and emotions and becoming a much better listener. Listening skills help you as a leader because they make your followers more interested in expressing their opinions and concerns to you. A good leader should be open on the ears to any changes that need to be made or suggestions that need to be heard. Putting yourself in their shoes shows them that you are also wise and, in the long run, the trust you build is priceless.

Chapter 11

How Emotional Intelligence Affects Your Motivation

Emotional intelligence positively increases your ability to self-motivate, which leads to living a better life and growing your career more quickly: the self-awareness and emotional skills of people who have high EQ shine positive sunshine on their motor skills. Sometimes, when we've had little motivation for a long draw, it's hard to get motivated again, kind of like taking a cheat day that turns into a cheat week. We are merely human, so this is natural for us. We want more than we can quickly get, but we don't feel the motivation to try hard to get what we want. The traits of an emotionally intelligent person who labels them as self-motivators and go-getters can be found in this chapter. Read on and ask yourself if you feel any of these traits describe you.

Motivated people set goals, and whenever they find themselves in crisis, they wonder why this is. Maybe the things that are happening in your life right now are making you too busy even to think you are positive. Or perhaps you don't get enough sleep.

Either way, you can get out of that crisis. Setting a goal and achieving it is excellent. Goals help us focus our attention on the most important things, such as the ultimate goal. It's also easier to know for sure what you want when you focus on a single goal. Freelance motivation is pretty tricky, so make it easier by becoming a goal setter and a go-getter!

Motivated people also seek inspiration. One of the most significant impulses for anyone is something that truly inspires them deep inside. Look for someone who can be a good role model or idol and listen to the words they say. You can often find motivational speeches and inspiring stories easily on video streaming services. Emotional intelligence helps us get inspired because people with higher EQs are more profound thinkers. They can appreciate the beauty of things that others may not always see. You can find inspiration everywhere if you look for it and sincerely hope to find it. It's an incredibly positive trait to have to be able to locate inspiration wherever you are.

Be enthusiastic about achieving your goal. Do your best to feel and show enthusiasm. If someone is telling you that they don't feel it or don't trust the process anymore, ask them to keep moving forward and be confident. As already mentioned, finding your inspiration can be the thrust inside you that makes you excited to wake up every morning and turn on the coffee machine, excitement is a powerful emotion that makes us do things we never thought humanly possible. , because it makes our blood pump and our adrenaline flows through our bodies.

Anticipate the result. This might sound difficult, and many people just ignore it as if it didn't matter. But it works. Help people are struggling with nicotine addiction to quit smoking after many attempts. Help people cut alcohol out of their lives. Building the anticipation for the result is done by thinking about what it will be like finally after winning. If you find inspiration and want to start working towards one of your goals, don't start right away. Many of us will get excited and in a hurry and want to get started as soon as possible. This can be the end of it all, though. Set a future date and set it as the start date. Mark the calendar appropriately. Create excitement for that date, then make it seem like it's the most important date of the month.

Make your goal achievable and remind yourself of it every day. Maybe write it on a post-it and stick it on the fridge, or you could write it on a whiteboard. Either way, you should do your best to remind yourself of your goal every day. It may even benefit you to post your goal online on social media so your colleagues can help you hold yourself accountable. If you were trying to lose weight, maybe create a weight loss chart and put it on your bathroom door as long as Think about your goal every day and ask for support. Perhaps talking about your goal will help you achieve it. You can always find someone who will support you, even on social media.

Realize that motivation isn't a steady stream of secure personal support. There may be times when you find that your motivation is superficial. It comes and goes. This is one of the reasons why self-motivation is so important to you to be able to achieve. When you feel tired of your goals, or just plain weak and exhausted, there won't always be someone next to you with a bottle of water telling you to come back there. You have able to get on the plate and swing on your own sometimes. It's okay to get tired, and it's okay to want to quit, but it's not okay to let those feelings push your feet to the ground. Motivation won't make you feel like sunshine and rainbows all the time; it just helps you get started.

Stay faithful and never give up. If you have to stop, make sure you stop because you have to, not because you chose to. These are your goals. These are your dreams. Stick to them firmly, because life on this Earth is short and you may not have another chance as good as the one you have. Don't be discouraged. You may not feel motivated today, and you may have to force yourself on and on your feet, but you better grit your teeth and stick. The motivation will return. It may come back a week or a month later, but it will come back. Your goal is a mile-long journey, and this little spot where you don't feel motivated is just a bump in the road. You have to walk this road like a wave across the ocean, facing all the ups and downs.

Now since we talked about all this emotion and the tsunami that can be, the discouragement may come from your goals being too big at first. It would be like saying: "my goal is to become a doctor". Without first starting with "I want to get my degree". Start with smaller goals and achieve them individually. That way, you have a plan. However, don't allow yourself to get lazy and use your more modest goals as an excuse to work easier. You don't have to start by doing super intense workouts every day of the week, you can just start small and work until you do what's comfortable for you, but again, don't let these smaller goals be your excuse to refrain from pushing yourself.

Once you start building on these little successes, you will learn how rewarding they are. You can't fail if you start somewhere easy enough that you are sure to be successful. Once you've mastered that goal, hit the next one, then the future, and then keep chasing it. After a while, you will be able to look back on everything you have done and see how far it has taken you. Don't forget to share your successes with others as well. All of these positive things will help you learn how to motivate yourself. Not to mention, by taking small steps, you are far less likely to fail.

Now there is some time to take a break and read your goals. Look at the finished product often, as this will motivate you. Remind yourself to keep watching it and never forget why you started here. You started here because of that goal, so take a look at how to achieve it as hard as possible.

Also, maybe join an online forum or social media group to surround yourself with people who share similar goals to yours. These people are the ones who will help you get through those bumps on the road. Thanks to them for that. You're going to need a fantastic support group, and those kinds of people most likely have a lot of experience where you lack them. Let them know that you are near or far from your goal and remember to ask for help. They may be telling you things you can't hear anywhere else, and they may have that vital hint that you never knew is an absolute game-changer.

So no, you're getting close to reaching your goal. Do your best not to stop and focus on the difficulties, focus on the reward you have coming for you in the end. There is more to life things we find challenging to overcome, but those rare rewards in the end that are the kind of rewards that make us think about our hard work, those are precious. This is a valuable piece of life that you should never let anyone take away from you. When you commit, you can do anything. You should aim high and work hard because one day you will wake be better than you.

Lastly, don't let negative thoughts prevail over positive ones due to lack of character. This isn't easy for anyone, and no matter how others have made it look, don't be fooled by the very particular parts of the process that you have been shown. Everyone struggles with something, and everyone who has achieved your goal has probably worked their fingertips for it. Replace your negative thoughts with those and watch your motivation take off. There is no negativity when you can shed light on any situation because even failure can be seen as an opportunity to learn.

Chapter 12

Managing Stress The Smart Way

Healthily managing stress is part of building your emotional intelligence. Stress management is essential for your mental and emotional health, as it provides an outlet for the negative feelings you have collected during your day/week/year. This is why people often say, "I need a vacation!" You need a break from time to time because life is stressful for everyone. Working for long periods without interruption is a direct blow to grumpiness or, worse, depression. Also, don't let anyone tell you that you take too many breaks or too many vacations. We are on this Earth only once, so make your life the best possible version and ENJOY life. Let's talk about stress management.

First, you should avoid things that amplify stress like nicotine, caffeine, and excessive alcohol. Coffee in the morning isn't a bad idea, but drinking it to excess can lead to daytime fatigue that accompanies a harsh caffeine crash. Those are the worst. Maybe try eating a healthier breakfast with things that give you energy like eggs, milk, fruit, or granola.

As for alcohol, there is nothing wrong with using alcohol as a tool to relax, but in excess, we all know what comes next. Hangover. Hangovers make you feel super fatigued and very stressed, often with vomiting and headaches. Maybe opt for a glass of wine or a couple of beers instead of mixed spirits.

Avoid nicotine altogether if you can, as nicotine has been scientifically proven not what you want, instead.

And the action of smoking or chewing. We understand that smoking is a break to smoke and we enjoy time outdoors relaxing by sucking and exhaling, but the truth is that nicotine gives you a headache and drains your energy. We do not forget that tobacco products often lead to serious health problems such as fatal cases of cancer.

Secondly, you could try relieving some stress in a way that benefits your body physically too! Yes, I'm talking about exercise. Exercise isn't that bad if you think about it, because you can always go at your own pace and you don't even need equipment. You can find training videos online very quickly, and most of them don't require you to own something super special. Try going for a walk, doing squats, jumping jacks, or pushups, whatever you can do using your body. Many people find the type of sport they practise, such as boxing or shooting, ways to deal with stress-related specifically to anger.

Thirdly, try to sleep well. Not everyone gets to sleep through the night, sure, but you need to take the time to rest a reasonable amount. Going too long without sleep leads to severe fatigue and even illness. It may be tempting to stay up late because you feel like the night is your only free time, but if that's the case, you need to tweak your schedule to take more breaks in life seriously. Money and bills are part of being an adult and are very important, but living your life to pay the bills and die is not ideal for anyone. So put that phone down, turn off the TV, and sleep tight!

Now that you've exercised slept, and changed your diet, perhaps try a relaxation technique you've never tried before, such as yoga, baking, art, or drinking hot tea on the back porch. There are many things that you probably haven't tried, such as self-hypnosis or meditation. You might think of a self-calm mantra-like, "Everything will be fine." or "A bad day not a bad life". Maybe it's time you took that old instrument you haven't played in years out of the closet and blow some dust off. There's no need to be afraid of new things, just dip your foot in the water and see if you like it!

Also, try talking about your feelings with someone you trust. In this book, I've talked about how important it is to interact with others about your feelings. It allows you to let off steam and clear your mind of any anger or negative emotions. Being stressed can affect things like judgment and attitude, and as long as you interact with others, they will be able to tell that something is wrong with you. Ask them for their views on the issues that are stressing you out and let them tell you how they think you should handle it. You may not take their advice, but you should at least be open to it.

Have you ever tried keeping a diary? Writing down what stresses you and writing about your problems helps you refresh yourself after a hard day. The great thing about journals is that they don't tell your secrets, so you can write whatever you want. You could write about someone giving you a headache, or you could write what you wish you could tell them. It is similar to writing an angry letter and throwing it away.

Magazines are very therapeutic and provide relief from having to keep your mouth shut and thoughts for you. They are a window of expression, and you can get creative with them. You may be attracting stress instead of writing, lyrics or poetry.

Try to take control of the problems that are causing you stress. If you can identify the culprit, crush him. Sometimes we forget that we are responsible for our life and it becomes easy to react to our problems without thinking. It also becomes easier to feel helpless in our lives, but we are never hopeless. You can always ask for help, but you have to take that first action yourself. You have to be the first person to recognize the problem and decide that you want to do something about it. It is tough to help someone who does not wish to help.

Stress management is not a difficult thing to balance. All you need to remember to do is take breaks when you feel you need it and ask for help need it. Of course, a healthy, drug-free and alcohol-free diet always helps. Most importantly, you need to know that you need a bit of stress management now and then.

Conclusion

The activities we produce in our life are all largely according to ours emotions and emotional intelligence. It makes sense that when people have

a fantastic awareness of organizational and communication skills.

It will soon result in possessing the ability to make appropriate decisions as well interactions with other individuals. What we know from our emotions yes we try to pursue the lifestyle we would like to live and do more of what we have desire in our life, instead of what we don't do.

Emotional intelligence is a trait that can be continuously nurtured and augmented but with better awareness of this, individuals will be deficient worshiping friendships, inner fun and generally being relegated to live a life of non-social functions. Become more aware of the differences and impacts of eq and IQ often make us think that eq it is satisfactorily more significant than one's general intellect because being authentic with yourself may be the simplest way to live life better.

In this international era, it is vital to build a good sense of psychological conscience. After all, anyone who wishes to live a miserable life with not having the ability to usually share everything with the person we do love?